CONTEMPORARY LIVES

JUSTIN TIMBERLAKE

MUSICIAN, ACTOR, & DANCER

ABDO
Publishing Company

JUSTIN TIMBERLAKE

MUSICIAN, ACTOR, & DANCER

by Marcia Amidon Lusted

CREDITS

Published by ABDO Publishing Company, PO Box 398166, Minneapolis, Minnesota 55439. Copyright © 2012 by Abdo Consulting Group, Inc. International copyrights reserved in all countries. No part of this book may be reproduced in any form without written permission from the publisher. The Essential Library™ is a trademark and logo of ABDO Publishing Company.

Printed in the United States of America,
North Mankato, Minnesota
112011
012012

 THIS BOOK CONTAINS AT LEAST 10% RECYCLED MATERIALS.

Editor: Lauren Coss
Copy Editor: Amy Van Zee
Series design and interior production: Emily Love
Cover production: Marie Tupy and Kelsey Oseid

Library of Congress Cataloging-in-Publication Data
Lusted, Marcia Amidon.
  Justin Timberlake : musician, actor, & dancer / by Marcia Amidon Lusted.
      p. cm. -- (Contemporary lives)
  Includes bibliographical references and index.
  ISBN 978-1-61783-328-1
  1. Timberlake, Justin, 1981---Juvenile literature. 2. Rock musicians--United States--Biography--Juvenile literature. I. Title.
  ML420.T537L87 2012
  782.42164092--dc23
  [B]
                              2011040476

TABLE OF CONTENTS

Timberlake attended the 2011 Academy Awards when *The Social Network* was nominated for eight Oscars.

CHAPTER 1

In the
Spotlight

|||||||||||||||||||||||||||||||||||||||||||||||||

O n February 27, 2011, a limousine rolled up to the Kodak Theater in Los Angeles, California, for the Academy Awards presentation. With cameras flashing and fans cheering, Justin Timberlake stepped out onto the red carpet. Sporting a short haircut, a suit, and an easy smile, he made his way down the red carpet to the theater. His mom, Lynn Harless, accompanied him as his date for the evening. Timberlake attended the presentation because a movie he had costarred in, *The Social Network*, was nominated for eight Oscars. The movie won three Oscars that night. Several weeks earlier, it had won Best Motion Picture at the Golden Globe Awards.

Appearing at the Academy Awards, however, is just one of the things that has placed Timberlake in the spotlight. He was already a Grammy Award–winning singer and songwriter. He had received

THE ACADEMY AWARDS

In 1927, a group of 36 influential men and women in the movie industry created the Academy of Motion Picture Arts and Sciences, dedicated to the advancement of motion picture science and art. The Academy decided to create an award, known as the Academy Award, for outstanding achievement in different areas of moviemaking. Winners receive a golden statue officially called The Academy Award of Merit, also known as an Oscar. The Oscar statue is a knight standing on a reel of film and holding a sword. The first awards ceremony took place in 1929 at one of the Academy's banquets, with just 270 people attending at a cost of five dollars each. Since that first awards ceremony, more than 2,700 Oscar awards have been presented. The Academy Award of Merit is still considered the highest award for those who work in the movie industry.

One of Timberlake's many films in 2010 was *Yogi Bear*, in which Timberlake did the voice of the character Boo Boo.

Emmy Awards for his guest appearances acting in the popular late-night comedy/variety television show *Saturday Night Live*. Timberlake had also been in a number of other movies, including doing the voices for characters in *Shrek the Third* and *Yogi*

The Social Network is a 2010 movie about the founding of the social networking site Facebook and its creator Mark Zuckerberg. In the film, Timberlake portrays Napster cofounder Sean Parker as a greedy opportunist. The real Parker considered Timberlake's portrayal inaccurate, calling *The Social Network* "a complete work of fiction."[1]

Bear. Timberlake is well known for the charities he created and raised money for, as well as starting his own record label. He had begun producing, and sometimes writing, songs for recording artists such as Ciara and Leona Lewis. Timberlake is definitely a superstar, but he does not fit in to just one category. He is a singer, songwriter and producer, television actor, movie star, and businessman.

|||||||||||||||||||||||||||||||||||||||||||||||||||||

A NEW YEAR

The year 2011 would be one that held many new ventures and opportunities for Timberlake. In addition to his role as Napster creator Sean Parker in *The Social Network*, Timberlake had been involved in many other movies that were completed, ready for release, or about to start filming. The comedy movie *Bad Teacher*, starring Timberlake and actress Cameron Diaz, opened in June 2011. While it received a mixed response in the United States, the film became popular in Germany after its European debut. In addition, Timberlake starred with actress Mila Kunis in the romantic comedy *Friends with Benefits*, which opened in July. A third movie, *In Time*, is a futuristic thriller that opened in October, with Timberlake in the lead role. With these three movies, Timberlake had steadily climbed into starring roles rather than his previous roles as a supporting actor.

In 2011, Timberlake was a frequent guest host on *Saturday Night Live*. Not only did he act in various skits, he also wrote songs to accompany them. That year, Timberlake received Emmys for his role as a guest actor on the show and for his original music and lyrics written for the show. In 2007 and 2009, he had also received Emmys for his work on *Saturday Night Live*.

But Timberlake was involved in more than just music, television, and movies. He was also becoming more visible as a businessman and

Timberlake was a frequent guest on *Saturday Night Live*. In 2009 and 2011, he won Emmys for his role as a guest actor.

product spokesman. His line of fashion clothing was being sold by the department store Target. He had become the new brand ambassador for the automobile company Audi. He was also rumored to be part of a group of investors who were going to buy the social networking site MySpace. On top of this, Timberlake continued to work for several different charities and causes, including raising money for music education and for Shriners Hospitals for Children.

However, for the Timberlake fans who knew him first for his music, 2011 was a year of questions. They wondered if he had given up on his music career.

||||||||||||||||||||||||||||||||||||||||||||||||||||||||||||||||

A RETURN TO MUSIC?

Perhaps the best news for Timberlake's music fans in 2011 was the rumor that he would soon be returning to the recording studio to make his long-awaited third album. He had taken a break from his musical career after the release of his second album in 2006, and fans who knew him as a musician had been clamoring for new material. In March 2011, Timberlake told *Entertainment Weekly*:

> *I'm planning to spend some time in the studio this summer. I feel like I'm always writing music*

NOT FACEBOOKING ||||||||||||||||||||||||||||||||||||||||||||||||||||||||||||||||||||||||||||||||||||||||

Television host Ryan Seacrest interviewed Timberlake on the red carpet at the 2011 Academy Awards. Seacrest asked him, "When you took on this role [in *The Social Network*], you weren't Facebooking and you're not Facebooking now . . . is there a point when you thought of doing it?" Timberlake replied, "Not so much. I don't know. I'm really not that smart at it. I'm not savvy at it. Um, but I don't get a lot of free time and if I do, I would most likely be wanting to be golfing or snowboarding."[2]

and working on songs. But to make an album, you have to find a group of songs that speak to something that might not be on the radio currently and make sense for you personally.[3]

However, in June 2011, music fans had their hopes dashed again. In an interview Timberlake gave with another magazine, he said,

I don't have a single song ready to go. . . . Music is not my focus right now. It may be someday. It could happen next month or next year but right now it's not where it's at for me.[4]

|||||||||||||||||||||||||||||||||||||||||||||||||||||||||||

WHERE TO?

It seemed Timberlake's music career was going to continue to take a secondary role to his acting career. He was getting more movie roles—and more leads—as well as good reviews from critics. Would he completely quit the music business? He had first become famous because of his ability to sing and dance. As a member of the boy band *NSYNC, which released its first US album in 1998, Timberlake had become a pop music star

Timberlake got his start as a musician, but in more recent years, music seemed to take a backseat to the performer's acting and other ventures.

and heartthrob. When he moved into a solo pop career in 2002, he gained even more fans.

Clearly Timberlake owed his present career to music. But just how did music first start him on the path to superstardom? How did a regular kid from a town in Tennessee become one of the biggest names in both the music business and in Hollywood?

||||||||||

Justin frequently returns to Memphis, Tennessee. In 2006, he performed on the city's famous Beale Street.

CHAPTER 2

Tennessee Roots

||||||||||||||||||||||||||||||||

J ustin Randall Timberlake was born on January 31, 1981, in an era when pop music was changing and evolving. The television music network MTV debuted in August of that same year. Justin was born in a place known for its music history: Memphis, Tennessee. It would almost seem that Justin was born to be part of the musical world.

||||||||||||||||||||||||||||||

MEMPHIS

Memphis is known for its strong musical roots, especially rock and roll, rockabilly, and blues music. It calls itself the "Birthplace of Rock and Roll," the "Center of Soul," and the "Home of the Blues." It has produced great musicians, including Elvis Presley, Johnny Cash, Jerry Lee Lewis, B. B. King, and W. C. Handy. Memphis is home to the famous Beale Street and Elvis's former home, Graceland.

A MUSICAL FAMILY

Justin's family surrounded him with music. His mother, Lynn, played several different musical instruments, and his father, Randall (known as Randy), was a bluegrass singer and led a church choir. His grandfather, William (Bill) Bomar, was a guitarist. With so much music in his family, it was not surprising that Justin began singing at an early age.

Justin's favorite childhood toys were musical instruments, especially a plastic toy guitar. He liked to watch music videos of Michael and Janet Jackson, playing the videos over and over until he could copy the choreography exactly. His father and uncle played in a band, and whenever Justin

As a child, Timberlake loved to watch videos of singer Janet Jackson and her brother Michael performing. As an adult, Timberlake would perform with Janet Jackson.

attended the concerts, he stood right in front of the stage. His mother remembers,

> [He'd be] looking up at them as if he were in a trance. He would scream bloody murder when we had to drag him away from the stage. I guess it was just a sign![1]

Justin was a regular kid in many ways. His favorite food was pizza, and his favorite cartoon was *Inspector Gadget*. And like many kids, he dealt with the breakup of his parents' marriage. His parents had married very young—Justin's mother was 20 when he was born—and when Justin was three, his mother and father divorced. Two years later, his mother remarried to Paul Harless, a banker. They moved to Millington, a Memphis suburb in an area known as Shelby Forest. Justin grew up in a solid middle-class home and got along well with his stepfather. Justin's father, Randy, also

JUSTIN'S ANGEL ||||||||||||||||||||||||||||||||||||||||||||||||||||||||||||||||||||||||

In addition to having two half brothers, Justin also had a half sister named Laura Katherine, the first child of his father and his stepmother, Lisa. Laura died a few minutes after her birth on May 14, 1997. Justin mentions her in the liner notes for the first *NSYNC album, calling her "my angel in heaven."[2]

Justin attended E. E. Jeter Elementary School
in the Memphis suburb of Millington.

remarried and had two more sons, Justin's half
brothers, Jonathan and Stephen.

SCHOOL DAYS

Justin's elementary school years were not perfect.
He attended E. E. Jeter Elementary School in
Shelby Forest, where he was teased because he had
very curly hair and acne. He was called names such
as "pizza face."[3] Like many kids who are teased,
Justin found activities that made him happy,
including sports and singing. He played basketball,

Star Search was the first of the television talent competitions that would later lead to shows such as *American Idol*. Produced from 1983 to 1995, and again from 2003 to 2004, the show screened potential contestants through auditions. Contestants who passed the screening would appear on the show in different categories such as vocalists, dancers, and comedians. A panel of judges voted for the winner in each category by awarding the contestants stars based on their performances, with a maximum of four stars possible. The winner would then move on to later shows until competing in a semifinal show for the chance to win $100,000.

but he also began taking piano and voice lessons. After his mother videotaped Justin's performance in a third grade school talent show, singing teacher Bob Westbrook agreed to take him on as a student. Singing lessons taught Justin how to breathe properly while singing, stay on pitch, project his voice, and most important, have a good stage presence. Justin joined the Bob Westbrook Singers and gained performance experience with them.

Voice lessons gave Justin the confidence to begin entering talent shows and pageants. When he was ten, he won the 1991 Preteen Mr. America pageant, and a year later, he was the first male ever to win the Universal Charm Pageant. So it seemed like the next logical step was to audition for *Star Search,* a television talent show.

Justin's mother had learned that *Star Search* was holding auditions at a mall in Memphis, and it seemed like a good way to advance Justin's career. Competing against 500 other contestants, Justin won the chance to appear on the television show. He spent a great deal of time rehearsing before traveling to Orlando, Florida, where the show was taped. In 1993, at age 11, Justin appeared on *Star Search* under the name "Justin Randall." He sang country songs and received three and one-quarter stars from the judges. However, his competitor, a ten-year-old girl, received four stars.

It was a difficult loss to accept. Justin and his mother left Orlando and returned home. They could not have imagined that the defeat would turn out to be Justin's lucky break.

||||||||||||

Justin, *back row, third from left*, broke into music and acting with Disney's *The All New Mickey Mouse Club* when he was 12 years old.

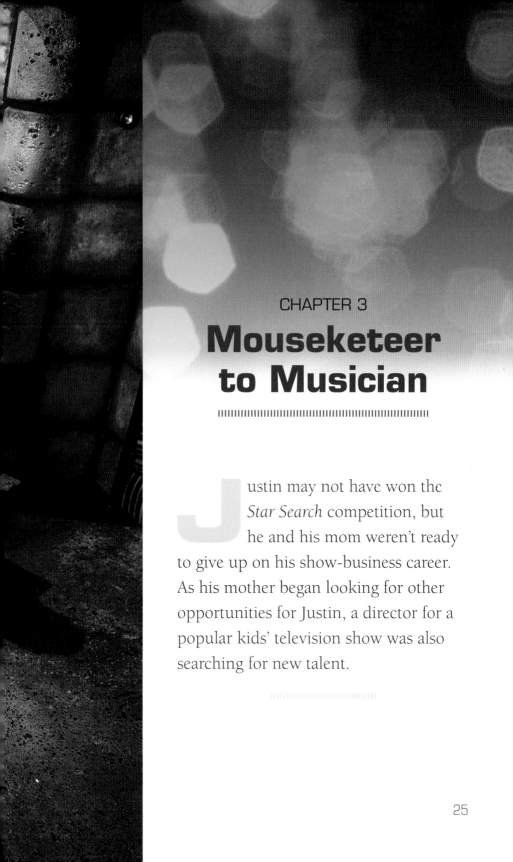

CHAPTER 3

Mouseketeer to Musician

|||||||||||||||||||||||||||||||||||||||||||||||||||||||||||||||||

Justin may not have won the *Star Search* competition, but he and his mom weren't ready to give up on his show-business career. As his mother began looking for other opportunities for Justin, a director for a popular kids' television show was also searching for new talent.

|||||||||||||||||||||||||||||||||

A LONG TRADITION

Director Matt Casella was involved in *The All New Mickey Mouse Club*, a popular Disney show that aired on ABC. However, the show's idea was not new. Its origins went back to the 1950s and the very first version of the show, *The Mickey Mouse Club*, which Walt Disney Productions created in 1955 and ran for four years. *The Mickey Mouse Club* was a variety show containing a mix of different types of segments, such as cartoons, singing and dancing, and comedy. The cast of the original *The Mickey Mouse Club* was made up of teenagers known as Mouseketeers.

The show was brought back again in 1977. Disney attempted to make it feel more contemporary by using popular music—which at that time was disco music—and more diverse cast members. But this version of *The Mickey Mouse Club* was never as popular as the original show and was discontinued after less than a year.

Even though the second version of the show had not been successful, Disney was persistent. It launched *The All New Mickey Mouse Club*, a new version that ran from 1989 to 1994. Most people called the show the *MMC*. This version of the show not only ran longer and was more popular than the second version, but it launched the careers of several of its young performers.

||||||||||||||||||||||||||||||||||||||||||||||||||||||||

CASTING CALL

Since 1988, Casella had been on a national search for the newest cast of Mouseketeers. He said he was searching for "normal kids with an extraordinary talent . . . not showbiz kids with agents."[1] Casella held auditions in many US cities, including Pittsburgh, Atlanta, and Nashville.

"On the drive back home from Florida, we saw a commercial on a motel TV for auditions for the Mickey Mouse Club the next day in a town called Hendersonville, Tennessee. . . .We went to some random office space, and I danced to an MC Hammer song."[2]

—JUSTIN TIMBERLAKE RECALLING HIS MMC AUDITION

Hundreds of kids were competing for the chance to appear on the show, but Justin made it

During his two years on the *MMC*, Justin, *center*, gained experience acting, singing, and dancing.

through the first round of auditions. In the next round, Justin had to sing, dance, and perform a speech. Soon he was hired as part of a group of new cast members Casella was adding to the existing cast of Mouseketeers. In 1993, Justin and his mother moved to Orlando, where the show was taped. Justin's show-business career was on its way.

ON THE SET

Becoming part of a television show and spending time on the set was a new experience for 12-year-old Justin. Most of the cast members were very young—between 11 and 18—and by law they had to attend school on the set for three hours every morning. Afternoons were spent in makeup, wardrobe, and rehearsing the show's musical numbers and skits. Then the show was taped in front of a live studio audience. It was hard work and a busy schedule, but because the cast members were together so much, they formed close relationships. Justin remembered spending time with Ryan Gosling, a fellow cast member who

MOUSEKETEERS

Other members of *The All New Mickey Mouse Club* cast would go on to become famous performers. These include singers Britney Spears, Christina Aguilera, and J. C. Chasez, actor Ryan Gosling, and actress Keri Russell. It is rumored that singer Jessica Simpson and actor Matt Damon were rejected after they auditioned for the *MMC*.

is now a famous movie actor. "Ryan and I used to steal golf carts and go driving in the middle of the park to get milk shakes, and we never got in trouble for it," he said. "We thought we were big [stuff]."[3]

Justin loved performing on the *MMC*, and he lived in Orlando from April through September, while the show was taping. He spent two seasons on the show and fully expected to return for a third season. Then, in February 1995, Disney unexpectedly announced that the *MMC* was being canceled. Most of the show's young cast was devastated.

Justin returned to his Tennessee home. He had learned a great deal about show business during his two years on the *MMC*, and once he was home, he continued performing in local school and community events. But Justin clearly felt frustrated by his sudden return to everyday life. He convinced his mom they should move to Los Angeles, California, so he could start trying out for roles in television sitcoms. His mother agreed, but just before they were set to move, another opportunity came along that would be even bigger than *The All New Mickey Mouse Club*.

BUILDING A BAND

In August 1995, Justin received a phone call from Chris Kirkpatrick, a singer whom Justin had previously met at auditions in Orlando. Kirkpatrick had been working with Lou Pearlman, a businessman who was active in the entertainment industry and specialized in putting together new bands. Pearlman had already created a pop band called the Backstreet Boys. While the band wasn't as well known as it would one day be, the group's popularity was gaining momentum.

Kirkpatrick had been a potential candidate for the Backstreet Boys, but he didn't make the final cut into the group. He suggested to Pearlman that they could form another five-person band, and Pearlman asked him to find some possible band

BEATING THE COMPETITION

In 2002, Pearlman wrote his autobiography *Bands, Brands, and Billions*. In the book, he compares the Backstreet Boys to the soft drink brand Coca-Cola. "If Backstreet turns out to be a dominant brand like Coke, someone is going to come along and create a Pepsi. We might as well beat them to it."[4] This was his explanation for starting *NSYNC when he had already started the Backstreet Boys, which people might have seen as competing with himself.

The Backstreet Boys, a popular boy band from the 1990s, paved the way for *NSYNC.

members. Kirkpatrick knew Justin loved to sing and perform, so he asked Justin if he was interested in auditioning for the new group. Justin was, and immediately flew down to Orlando again with his mother and stepfather.

Justin saw another familiar face at the tryouts for the new band. J. C. Chasez had been on *The All New Mickey Mouse Club* with Justin, and like Justin, he was a good singer and dancer. The two young men auditioned for Kirkpatrick and Pearlman and joined the new group. Now, with three members

The Backstreet Boys group was created in Orlando in 1993, and their first album debuted in 1996. The original members of the group were Nick Carter, A. J. McLean, Howie Dorough, Brian Litrell, and Kevin Richardson. The group had a three-year hiatus from 2001 to 2005. In 2006, Richardson left the band. But the remaining four members of the Backstreet Boys were still together and still performing as of 2011.

on board, the band needed just two more. Singer Joey Fatone became part of the group, as well as singer Jason Galasso, who soon quit the band because he felt it wasn't working. Westbrook, still Justin's vocal teacher, recommended Lance Bass, and soon Bass had replaced Galasso.

The band had its members. Now it needed a name. One night, the band, along with Pearlman and Justin's mother and stepfather, were eating at a restaurant. Pearlman recalled, "Lynn was talking and said, 'You know, these guys just sound so tight together, they sound very much in sync.'"[5] The boys were being noticed for their ability to sing in tight harmony, which did make them sound synchronized. Everyone agreed that *NSYNC sounded like a possible name for the group.

*NSYNC is often referred to as a "boy band," which is a term for a musical group that consists of only male singers. The members are expected to dance as well as sing, and their dance routines are often highly choreographed. They rarely play instruments when they perform or record, instead concentrating on singing and dancing. Rather than a group of musicians who choose to come together to make music, talent producers create most boy bands by auditioning members. These groups are commercial in nature and usually aimed at an audience of preteen or teen girls. Boy bands were very popular in the 1980s and 1990s, but they existed long before that. Early examples include barbershop quartets of the late nineteenth century and 1960s groups such as the Monkees. Boy bands continue today with groups including Big Time Rush and Mindless Behavior.

*NSYNC could also be created by using the last letter of each original member's first name: Justin, Chris, Joey, Jason, and J. C. The name *NSYNC was chosen.

||||||||||||||||||||||||||||||||||||||||||||||||||||||||

ON THEIR WAY

The band had five members and a name. Now it was time to start working on the group's vocal

Left to right: Justin Timberlake, Chris Kirkpatrick, Joey Fatone, J. C. Chasez, and Lance Bass made up the band *NSYNC.

skills, creating music, and getting the right people to notice the band. All five members were on the brink of a popularity bigger than they had ever imagined.

||||||||||

Justin had launched his career on the *MMC*, but his time with the boy band *NSYNC would make him a star.

CHAPTER 4

*NSYNC

||||||||||||||||||||||||||||||||||||||||||||||||||||||||

Pearlman had big plans for *NSYNC. He rented a house in Orlando for the five group members to live in. To get ready to make public appearances, the young men began rehearsing dance routines, working on their voices, and harmonizing together.

Pearlman hired Johnny Wright, the manager of the Backstreet Boys, to also manage *NSYNC. Wright set up several smaller concerts for the band.

The group's very first appearance was at Pleasure Island, a resort in Florida, on October 22, 1995. The concert was taped so the band could use it as a demonstration for record companies.

Soon the band auditioned for the executives at BMG, a large record company. The executives had a few concerns about the group. Bass's dancing abilities were not as strong as the other members and BMG was also uncertain about the group's name. But the executives finally decided to sign the band, with its current name, to the record company BMG Ariola Munich. *NSYNC's first record would be launched in Germany.

BUILDING A FAN BASE

After signing with BMG Ariola Munich, the *NSYNC members traveled to Sweden to work on their first album. The album's lead single "I Want You Back" was released in Germany on October 7, 1996, and by November 18, it was on Germany's top-ten songs list. *NSYNC began touring, first in Germany and then in other parts of Europe. The band's first album, *NSYNC*, was released on May 26, 1997, again in Germany. It climbed the record charts to Number 1 just two weeks after its release. Several other songs from the album made it onto the charts in other European countries. After seeing *NSYNC at a concert in Budapest, Hungary, an American representative for RCA Records, Vincent DiGiorgio, signed the band to the RCA label to produce the record in the United States.

*NSYNC's first US single, also "I Want You Back," debuted in the United States on January 20, 1998. It reached Number 13 on *Billboard* magazine's Hot 100 list. On March 24, the group's

BILLBOARD ||||||||||||||||||||||||||||||||||||||||||||||||||||||||||||||||||||||||||||||||||||||||||||||||

Billboard magazine, which is now considered to be the top magazine of the music industry, began publication in 1894. The publication got its name because it was originally intended as a magazine for the bill-posting industry—people who traveled around the country hanging advertising bills and posters.

The magazine expanded to include those who were involved with traveling circuses, fairs, and other shows. Eventually, in 1961, *Billboard* magazine became two separate magazines: one for those involved in traveling shows, called *Amusement Business*, and one for the music industry, called *Billboard Music Week*. *Billboard* is now read in more than 100 countries around the world, has its own entertainment awards, and has charts that track the popularity of new songs and albums.

first US album, also titled *NSYNC*, was released. It was not popular right away, but then the album got some help from a little Disney-style publicity.

||||||||||||||||||||||||||||||||||||||||||||||||||||||||||

THANKS TO THE BACKSTREET BOYS

Disney wanted to give a concert at the MGM studios in Orlando on July 18, 1998. Disney first asked the Backstreet Boys to perform, but the group declined. The Backstreet Boys's refusal to play the Disney concert would ultimately be a lucky break for *NSYNC. When Disney offered the slot to *NSYNC, the new group gladly accepted the opportunity. It was familiar territory for Justin and Chasez, because they had filmed the *MMC* show at MGM studios. The concert was filmed and shown on television several times.

The effects were immediate. Three weeks before the concert took place, the first *NSYNC album was only at Number 85 on the *Billboard* top 200 albums chart. Three weeks after the concert, the album was at Number 9. *NSYNC* would eventually sell 10 million copies. When the band released a second single, "Tearin' Up My Heart," it

MTV, or Music Television, debuted on cable television in August 1981. The channel broadcast music videos for popular songs, which at first were simple and provided for free by record companies. Soon the music industry began to realize that they had an enormous promotional tool, and labels began to invest more money in making creative, interesting music videos, which were sometimes considered shocking. Eventually MTV added a variety of shows to the channel in addition to broadcasting music videos. The channel now sponsors two major awards, the MTV Music Video Awards and the MTV Movie Awards.

immediately became one of the most-played songs on the radio and soon appeared as a music video on MTV. *NSYNC was even invited to tour with singer Janet Jackson on her world tour in 1998.

In November 1998, *NSYNC released its second album, a holiday album titled *Home for Christmas*. More singles followed, and soon *NSYNC was headlining its own tour. Other opportunities began to come along for the band. The group performed in an episode of the television show *Sabrina the Teenage Witch* in February 1999. They contributed a song to the sound track of the animated movie *Pokémon: The*

*NSYNC's second US album was a holiday album, *Home for Christmas*.

First Movie. By the summer of 1999, *NSYNC was one of the hottest, most exciting pop bands in the country. Album sales and concert tickets were bringing in millions of dollars.

Justin recalled, "It was exciting that we were having so much success and we could do whatever we wanted."[1] However, as their popularity and earnings increased, the band began to believe it was not seeing its fair share of the profit.

A FAIR SHARE?

The members of *NSYNC began to suspect that Pearlman was taking more of their money than the one-sixth he was entitled to as their manager. Justin remembered,

> We always knew he [Pearlman] was a little off, but it wasn't until we got our first checks for an album that sold 12 million copies that we were like, "Hmm, does yours say the same thing? Is that missing a zero?"[2]

Eventually the members of *NSYNC sued Pearlman, claiming that he was actually taking as much as 50 percent of their earnings.

The band threatened to leave Pearlman and the RCA record company and sign with another. Pearlman and RCA countersued, demanding $150 million and the rights to use the band's name. The

The members of *NSYNC sued Pearlman and eventually left his management after they discovered he was taking more than his fair share of the band's profits.

suit was finally settled out of court, and *NSYNC went on to sign with Jive records instead. Pearlman would still receive some money from the group,

The Recording Academy gives out Grammy Awards every year for outstanding performers in many different kinds of music. Grammy Awards are considered the music industry's most prestigious awards, and the academy members vote to determine the awards' recipients. A Grammy Award is given for artistic or technical achievement, rather than sales or position on industry charts. *NSYNC was nominated for several Grammys throughout its time as a band, but never won. Justin went on to win six Grammys as a solo artist later in his career.

but he would no longer be personally involved with the band.

||||||||||||||||||||||||||||||||||||||||||||||||||||

AT THE TOP

At the turn of the new millennium in 2000, *NSYNC was as hot as it could possibly be. The band members were photographed for the cover of Rolling Stone magazine. They appeared on the television show Saturday Night Live. They were nominated for three Grammy Awards, the highest awards given in the music industry. They even appeared as cartoon versions of themselves on the animated television show The Simpsons. Justin in particular was receiving a great deal of attention in the media because of his relationship with pop singer Britney Spears. She had been one of the other cast members on the *MMC*, and she and Justin had remained friends. By 1999, Spears was building her own solo music career. She was the opening act for *NSYNC on its tour, and she and Justin had started dating. "We were two birds of the same feather—small-town kids, doing the same thing," Justin explained.[3]

*NSYNC had reached the peak of popularity. The band was in demand for concerts and television appearances. The members had performed at the Academy Awards, the World Series, the Olympics, and the Super Bowl. *NSYNC had recorded songs with other famous performers such as Aerosmith, Michael Jackson, and Stevie Wonder. By the end of 2000, the band would be the highest-earning pop music group in

JUSTIN AND BRITNEY ||||||||||||||||||||||||||||||||||||||||||||||||||||||||||||||||||||

Justin and Britney Spears first met on the *MMC* set in 1993. They remained friends after its cancellation and dated from 1999 to 2002. Their high-profile relationship was closely followed by paparazzi and the media because Britney was also a pop music superstar, popular with teenage and preteen girls.

Justin started dating Britney Spears, another pop star and former *MMC* cast member, in 1999. Their relationship was highly publicized.

the world, with $267 million in album and concert ticket sales. The question now was: where could *NSYNC possibly go from here?

||||||||||

By *NSYNC's third album, *No Strings Attached*, Timberlake had stepped into a greater leadership role in the band.

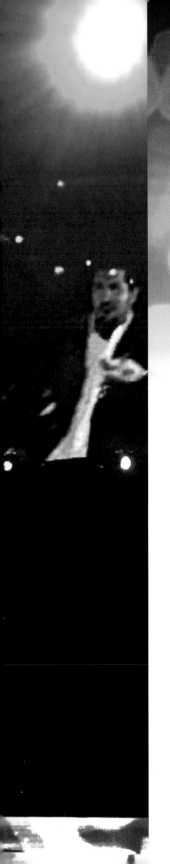

CHAPTER 5

A Changing Role

'N SYNC released its third album, *No Strings Attached*, on March 21, 2000. It sold more than 2 million copies in its first week and occupied the Number 1 spot on the *Billboard* charts for eight weeks. *No Strings Attached* became the top-selling album of 2000 and the best-selling album of its decade.

Timberlake expanded his role in creating the album. He wrote one of the songs, sang solo on two more, and even got involved with sound mixing. Later that year, the group traveled on a No Strings Attached Tour, and MTV made a special show about how *NSYNC prepared for their tour. The special became available on DVD, and the tour itself was featured as an HBO television special.

CELEBRITY

*NSYNC was preparing another album for release in January 2001, but the new album, *Celebrity*, was delayed until July. This time the band went in a different direction and had more creative participation. Chasez and Timberlake were particularly involved in making the album, with Timberlake cowriting seven of the songs. This album was more heavily influenced by musical

JUSTIN GRADUATES

Similar to many teens who become involved in show business, Timberlake never had an official high school graduation. He had worked with tutors instead of attending an actual high school. At an *NSYNC concert in Memphis in May 2000, two of Timberlake's tutors appeared and presented him with a cap, gown, and diploma.

*NSYNC's 2001 PopOdyssey Tour was an extremely complicated and visual show, with lights, smoke, lasers, and other special effects.

styles such as rhythm and blues (R & B) and hip-hop.

In May 2001, the band started a four-month tour to publicize the album before its release in July. The PopOdyssey Tour featured concerts in large stadiums. The tour was complicated and required 50 trucks and 24 buses to transport the people and equipment from show to show. The band members rode mechanical bulls, showed a computer-animated video, and set off lasers, smoke, and fireworks. A reviewer for MTV commented on Timberlake's role in the concert extravaganza:

[Timberlake has] always been a fan favorite, but it looks like his bandmates are finally giving him a larger share of the spotlight.[1]

Altogether, more than 2 million fans attended the concerts. The tour was reported to have taken in almost $1 million for each performance. However, fans weren't quite as receptive to this new sound from *NSYNC. Although *Celebrity* received generally good reviews, its sales were not as strong as previous albums.

HIATUS

In April 2002, the group decided to take a break from making records and performing. The members originally intended to resume their work that September, but in the meantime, there had been changes. Timberlake decided that he wanted to focus on his solo singing career. Bass was in Russia attending an astronaut program, although as of 2011 he had not gone into space. Both Bass and Fatone had indicated that they wanted to pursue acting careers.

The *NSYNC members still went to various events and awards shows together, but now no one was talking about resuming their work as a boy band. *NSYNC's last televised performance was at the 2003 Grammy Awards, where they sang a tribute to the pop group Bee Gees. The group's last public performance took place at the 2004 Annual Challenge for Children. They sang "The Star-Spangled Banner," which happened to be the first song the five of them had sung together.

The days of *NSYNC were over, but Timberlake was well on his way to a solo career. In August 2002, he moved to Los Angeles, and he and Spears ended their romantic relationship. He was 21 years

PLAYING WITH JAGGER ||||||||||||||||||||||||||||||||||||||||||||||||||||||||||||||||||||

In 2003, Timberlake performed in a benefit concert in Toronto, Canada. He was the only pop music star alongside famous rock and rollers such as Mick Jagger and AC/DC. In an interview with *Rolling Stone* magazine, Timberlake talked about how a crowd of Canadians who didn't like his music actually pelted him with water bottles. "It messed with my head for a good two weeks," he said. "But I saw it coming. I woke up that morning, and I said, 'I think these people who are coming to the show are just really going to hate me.' But when Mick Jagger asks you to come do a benefit concert, do you say no?"[2]

old and ready to change his image to go along with a new identity as a solo star.

||||||||||||||||||||||||||||||||||||||||||||||||||||||||||||||||

JUSTIFIED

Timberlake began recording a new album, but this time, it was as a solo artist. He wanted to continue using the R & B sound from the last *NSYNC album, so he asked R & B singer Brian McKnight to help him produce the album. Timberlake also enlisted the help of hip-hop producers The Neptunes, hip-hop artist and producer Timbaland, and Timbaland's fellow producer Scott Storch. Timbaland and Storch produced and arranged the music for the song "Cry Me a River," and Timberlake wrote the lyrics. Timberlake cowrote all 13 songs on the album. He premiered his first single from the album, "Like I Love You," at the MTV Music Video Awards in August 2002.

The album, *Justified*, was released on November 5. It was not as popular as the final *NSYNC album had been, but it still sold a respectable 3 million copies in the United States and more than 7 million copies worldwide. Timberlake went on tour to promote his album in May 2003.

In September 2003, the McDonald's fast-food chain announced a partnership with Timberlake. Timberlake agreed to sing the "I'm Lovin' It" jingle and appear in some of the company's television advertising. In turn, McDonald's agreed to sponsor Timberlake's 2003 European tour. A spokesperson for McDonald's commented, "Justin Timberlake is absolutely connected to today's consumer attitudes and trends. His cultural relevance is right in tune with McDonald's new direction."[4]

Gradually, his fans began to evolve from former *NSYNC fans to those who appreciated him for his new music. An article in *Rolling Stone* magazine in December 2003 even called Timberlake "the new king of pop," and he won three MTV Music Video Awards that year.[3] It seemed the transformation from boy-band star to solo performer was a success.

Timberlake showed he was capable of having his own career beyond *NSYNC. But those who thought he would be content to continue on as a musician only were underestimating him.

||||||||||

CBS criticized Timberlake and Jackson for their infamous wardrobe malfunction during their halftime show performance at the 2004 Super Bowl.

CHAPTER 6

New Directions

‖‖

With Timberlake's first solo album and concert tour behind him, it seemed his post-*NSYNC music career was already going strong. In February 2004, Timberlake and singer Janet Jackson were invited to perform during the halftime show of Super Bowl XXXVIII, which would be broadcast on CBS in front of a television audience of millions. At the end of their song, Timberlake was supposed to tear off part of Jackson's black leather costume. This was a planned move that went along with the song's lyrics and should have only revealed her pink undergarment. However, part of the costume actually came off, revealing Jackson's breast. Because the show was on live television, nothing could be edited. Both Timberlake and Jackson were criticized for the incident, which became known as a "wardrobe malfunction." Timberlake had long been a media favorite, but the Super Bowl incident put him in the media's crossfire more than ever.

Meanwhile, Timberlake felt harassed by the paparazzi who followed him and actress Cameron Diaz, whom he had started dating in 2003. The media frequently aired rumors about the couple and whether they were going to be married or

WARDROBE MALFUNCTION

After the Super Bowl incident, both Timberlake and Jackson were banned from appearing on the 2004 Grammy Awards show a week later unless they issued on-air apologies during the event. Timberlake did so as he received one of his two Grammy Awards for *Justified* that night, saying, "I know it's been a rough week on everybody. What occurred was unintentional, completely regrettable, and I apologize if you guys are offended."[1]

Timberlake and Diaz dated from 2003 to 2007.

break up. And they hounded Timberlake and Diaz, hoping for photos, a whiff of a scandal, or new information. In addition to his media issues, Timberlake also discovered that he needed to have surgery to remove nodules (benign growths) from his vocal cords. Nodules are common among singers, but Timberlake would be required to rest his voice for three months following the surgery. He was not allowed to sing or even speak loudly.

Like most celebrities, Timberlake has had to deal with the constant presence of paparazzi. The word refers to photojournalists who specialize in taking candid photographs of celebrities and selling the photos to magazines and newspapers. Often the more candid and revealing the photographs, the more the paparazzi get paid for them. As a result, these photojournalists trail celebrities constantly and often intrude on the privacy, and even the safety, of the people they stalk.

It seemed like a good time to take a break from the public eye and to pursue another one of his interests: becoming a movie actor.

||||||||||||||||||||||||||||||||||||||||||||||||||||||

ON THE SCREEN

Timberlake had already started his acting career with small roles in television shows such as *Touched by an Angel* in 1999 and the movie *Model Behavior* in 2000. He had a bigger role on the small screen when he hosted an episode of the television show *Saturday Night Live* on October 11, 2003, also appearing as the show's musical guest. He continued to make occasional cameo appearances on *Saturday Night Live* and was invited to host the show again in 2006.

That year also brought the US release of the film *Edison Force*, which was the first movie in which Timberlake had a lead role. The movie is about a young journalist (played by Timberlake) who discovers a group of corrupt policemen and teams up with an investigative reporter to expose them. The film, also starring actors Morgan Freeman and Kevin Spacey, was slated to be released in 2005. However, after the film received poor reviews in several test showings, the studio held it until 2006 and then released the movie right to DVD instead of showing it in theaters.

Timberlake appeared in three more movies in 2006: *Alpha Dog*, *Black Snake Moan*, and *Southland Tales*. Timberlake generally received good reviews for his acting. He went on to provide the voice of

"Justin Timberlake is terrific in this film. I told him it's time to stop singing."[2]

—*ACTOR BRUCE WILLIS ON TIMBERLAKE'S PERFORMANCE IN* ALPHA DOG

Artie in the animated movie *Shrek the Third*, which was released in 2007.

IIIIIIIIIIIIIIIIIIIIIIIIIIIIIIIIIIIIIIIIIIIIIIIIIIIIIIIIIII

STILL SINGING

Timberlake's interest in establishing a substantial film career made some fans of his music wonder if he was giving up on singing. But in December 2005, while still working on his acting career, he returned to the recording studio to work on his second solo album. Once again, Timbaland assisted him in creating an album with an R & B feel, but this new music also had more elements of hard rock and roll. The album, *FutureSex/LoveSounds*, was released in September 2006 to good reviews.

FutureSex/LoveSounds debuted at Number 1 on the *Billboard* 200 top albums chart, selling 684,000 copies in the first week after its release. Timberlake performed the album's lead single, "SexyBack," at the 2006 MTV Music Video Awards. "SexyBack" also spent seven weeks at Number 1 on the *Billboard* Hot 100 chart. Timberlake went on a world tour in January 2007 to promote his new album, and in 2008 he received two Grammy Awards for songs from the album.

IIIIIIIIIIIIIIIIIIIIIIIIIIIIIIIIIIIIIIIIIIIIIIIIIIIIIIIIIII

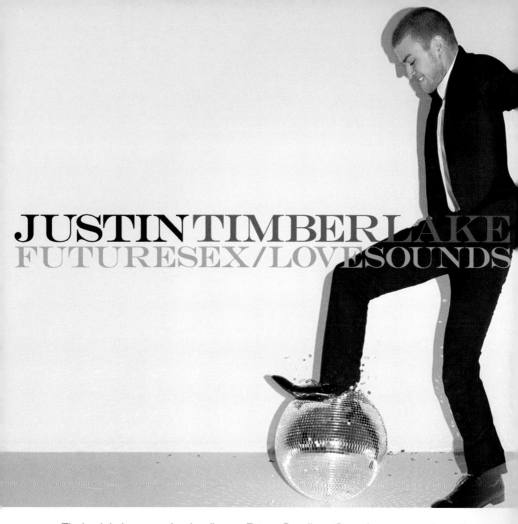

JUSTIN TIMBERLAKE
FUTURESEX/LOVESOUNDS

Timberlake's second solo album, *FutureSex/LoveSounds*, was nominated for four Grammys in 2007. Timberlake won two Grammys that year, one for Best Dance Recording and one for Best Rap/Sung Collaboration.

COLLABORATIONS

Timberlake seemed determined not to give up his music career. Throughout 2007 and 2008 he added vocals to songs on a variety of other performers' albums. In 2007, Timberlake cowrote, produced, and sang on two songs for the group Duran Duran's album *Red Carpet Massacre*. He also sang on one song on rapper 50 Cent's album *Curtis*. That December, Timbaland played a song called "4 Minutes" at Philadelphia's Jingle Ball, a major pop music concert held each year. It was an enticing taste of the song, a duet between pop superstar Madonna and Timberlake, which formally debuted on March 17, 2008. The song was part of Madonna's eleventh album, *Hard Candy*, and Timberlake had collaborated with her to write five songs on the album. Timberlake appeared in the music video, and he performed "4 Minutes" with Madonna on the Los Angeles portion of her tour. In November 2008, Timberlake released his own single "Follow My Lead," which was only available

THE PHONE

Timberlake produced a new MTV reality television show in 2009, *The Phone*. In it, four contestants accept a scavenger hunt-like mission via a cell phone call. In one such mission, a contestant was directed to crawl along the Seattle Space Needle. The contestants competed against each other to win a $50,000 prize at the end of six episodes. The show received mixed reviews from critics and did not run past the first season.

Timberlake starred with Jeff Bridges, *left*, in the 2009 movie *The Open Road*.

as a charitable download from MySpace to benefit Shriners Hospitals for Children.

However, Timberlake had not put acting aside completely. After finishing his 2007 tour for *FutureSex/LoveSounds*, he had signed up to act in two more movies: a comedy called *The Love Guru* and a drama called *The Open Road*. It was clear that Timberlake was not content to focus on just one aspect of his popularity. He already had careers in music and acting, but soon he would add even more ventures to his résumé.

||||||||||

*NSYNC's charity basketball game continued after the band broke up. Timberlake and then-girlfriend Diaz both played in the 2004 game.

Using His Fame for Good

||||||||||||||||||||||||||||||||||||||||||||||||||||

From his earliest days of fame as a member of *NSYNC, Timberlake was active in different kinds of charitable causes. He has continued to raise money for worthy causes throughout his career.

||||||||||||||||||||||||||||||||||||||||

NOT JUST A GAME

While he was still a member of *NSYNC, Timberlake combined his love of basketball with charity. The musical group sponsored an annual charity basketball game, holding the first game in Atlanta, Georgia, in August 1999. Several celebrity players joined *NSYNC on the court, including R & B artist and actor Usher and NBA star Kobe Bryant. The annual games continued for several years after *NSYNC's split. The proceeds benefited several children's charities, including *NSYNC's charity, The Challenge for Children Foundation, and Timberlake's charitable foundation, The Justin Timberlake Foundation. Timberlake's foundation was created specifically to raise money for music education programs in schools, although it has gradually expanded its focus to include raising funds for Shriners Hospitals for Children and a Memphis music museum.

At first, most of the people who attended the games were teenage girls who were fans of *NSYNC. The game continued as an annual event, even after *NSYNC disbanded. The group came back together to perform at the sixth annual event,

Timberlake's love of basketball didn't end with the *NSYNC charity games. When Timberlake moved to Los Angeles in August 2002, he continued to play basketball with the exclusive NBA Entertainment League, which included celebrities such as Tobey McGuire, Jamie Foxx, Ashton Kutcher, and Will Ferrell. The games were played at a school in Santa Monica, California, and were only open to family and friends of the players.

something they'd never done even when they were together.

||||||||||||||||||||||||||||||||||||||||||||||||||||||

AN ECO-FRIENDLY STAR

Timberlake continued to use his celebrity to try to improve the world around him. In 2005, the Recording Academy—the same organization that awards the Grammys—gave Timberlake a special humanitarian award for his work to promote and fund music education in his home state of Tennessee.

Timberlake also cared about the environment. After finishing his Australian music tour in November 2007, he donated $100,000 of his earnings to the Wildlife Warriors group. The group was founded by Steve Irwin, a naturalist and television host who died in 2006. In the fall of 2011, Timberlake was honored with the Futures Award by the Environmental Media Association (EMA). The EMA gives the award to people in entertainment it believes to be future environmental leaders. They gave it to Timberlake because of his efforts to reduce the carbon footprint of his tours, his continuous support for environmental issues, and his management of an eco-friendly golf course.

In 2007, Timberlake had purchased a golf course near his childhood home near Memphis and set out to make it environmentally friendly. He reportedly spent $16 million to buy and refurbish the course, which he named Mirimichi, a Native American word meaning "a place of happy retreat." Mirimichi is designed to be a green, or eco-friendly, golf course. Part of the course is a nature preserve with surrounding forests, native grassland, lakes, streams, and waterfalls. It is the first golf course to receive certification as an Audubon International Classic Sanctuary for the course's conservation, management of wildlife and habitats, and other environmental protection steps. Mirimichi, which

Timberlake is an avid golfer. He even owns his own golf course, Mirimichi.

opened in 2009, is only the ninth golf course
in the world to receive the Golf Environment
Organization certification for its environmentally
conscious use of water, pesticides, and energy.
Timberlake said of the golf course, "I think this is
probably the coolest thing I've ever been a part of
in my life."[1]

GOLFING FOR KIDS . . .
AND EVERYONE ELSE

Timberlake didn't just own a golf course—he
also loved to golf. In 2007, the Professional
Golfers Association (PGA) Tour announced

In December 2006, *Golf Digest* magazine issued a list of the top 100 golfers who were also musicians. Timberlake tied for fifteenth place alongside Darius Rucker of the band Hootie and the Blowfish and Jason Scheff from the group Chicago.

that in October 2008 Timberlake would begin hosting the Las Vegas, Nevada, stop on the golfing tour. Renamed The Justin Timberlake Shriners Hospitals for Children Open, the proceeds would benefit the children who receive free treatment at Shriners Hospitals around the country. Timberlake participated in the celebrity tournament that took place on the day before the professional tournament, and he also hosted a charity concert called Justin Timberlake and Friends in the week preceding the event. During 2009 alone, Timberlake's efforts on behalf of Shriners Hospitals for Children brought in more than $9 million. This was one of the largest sums of money ever raised by a US celebrity for a single charity.

|||||||||||||||||||||||||||||||||||||||||||||||||||||||

MONEY FOR MUSIC

Aside from sports, Timberlake's lifelong involvement in music has led him to support music in schools. The first donation made by The Justin Timberlake Foundation was to his old school. Through the foundation, Timberlake has also donated $200,000 to the Memphis Rock 'n' Soul Museum and the Memphis Music Foundation. The museum and foundation are dedicated to Memphis music history and promoting music education in schools. Timberlake said of his donation,

> Music education and keeping the legacy of Memphis Music alive has always been important to me. . . .That is why I will always continue to support my hometown the same way they have always supported me.[2]

Timberlake also joined the American Music Conference to promote the importance of music in schools, especially at a time when many music programs were being cut due to budget concerns.

From the start of his career, Timberlake worked to raise money for worthy causes. Although he had gotten his start in music, he was quickly proving himself to be a man of many talents and interests.

||||||||||

In 2007, Timberlake opened a Memphis-style restaurant called Southern Hospitality with friends Eytan Sugarman, *left*, and Trace Ayala, *right*.

CHAPTER 8

Timberlake the Businessman

|||||||||||||||||||||||||||||||||||||||||||||||||||||||||||||||||||||||

Timberlake was definitely not limiting himself to one career path. He continued collaborating with other musicians, writing songs for commercials and *Saturday Night Live* skits, and working with various charities. But he was also investing time and money in several business ventures that had nothing to do with music or acting.

|||||||||||||||||||||||||||||||

Timberlake's experience in owning Southern Hospitality has not always been easy. In November 2008 and May 2009 the restaurant was sued by employees. The first lawsuit was brought by an employee who claimed he was not fairly paid. He said the restaurant had not given him his share of the automatic gratuity that was added to each bill. He also claimed that he had often worked more than 40 hours in a week without receiving overtime pay. Then, in May 2009, a female manager at Southern Hospitality filed a sexual discrimination suit, claiming that she was subject to harassment while working at the restaurant and was fired when she complained. For both cases, it was never publicly known if the suits were settled out of court.

PUTTING HIS NAME ON IT

Since 2003, Timberlake had co-owned three different restaurants. Chi opened in West Hollywood, California, in 2003, but closed in 2005. In New York City, the Italian restaurant Destino opened in 2006 and Southern Hospitality opened in 2007. Southern Hospitality was a joint venture with Timberlake's childhood friends Juan "Trace" Ayala and Eytan Sugarman. The three men had grown up eating Southern-style foods, such as barbecue, in Memphis, and the project was an effort to bring these foods to New York City.

In addition to his other business ventures, Timberlake has his own fashion line, William Rast, with his friend Ayala.

Timberlake's clothing company, William Rast, sponsored a race car in 2011. In May, the car won the 2011 Indy 500 race. In response to the win, Timberlake posted on Twitter: "What a Memorial Day weekend! The William Rast car just won the Indy 500!"[2]

In another collaboration with his friend Ayala, Timberlake launched a clothing line. They called it William Rast clothing, naming it after their maternal grandfathers William Bomar and John Rast. In October 2006, the clothing line debuted at a fashion show in Los Angeles. Ayala described the type of clothing he and Timberlake had in mind for William Rast as "a little bit of Tennessee mixed with a little Hollywood flair" and inspired by Elvis.[1] Ayala said,

Elvis is the perfect mixture of Justin and I. You can go back and see pictures of him in cowboy boots and a cowboy hat and a nice button-down shirt, but then again you can see him in a tux and a collared shirt with rhinestones on it and slacks. We like to think "If he was alive today, what would he be wearing?"[3]

The clothing line grew, especially after the addition of new designers and the announcement that department store Target would carry the line in its stores.

But Timberlake wasn't just interested in investing in restaurants and fashion. In 2007, he launched his own record label, Tennman Records, in partnership with Interscope Records. The first four artists to be signed to Tennman Records were Matt Morris, Esmee Denters, Free Sol, and Bren. Timberlake was actively involved in the record label. He helped select and sign the new artists,

"Matt has been my friend since I was 11 years old. And we have a connection through music that is like nothing I have with anyone else on the planet. And we can go not seeing each other for 5–6 years and then sit down and write a song together and it would be something exceptional. He's like a chameleon: his music ability, knowledge, and application. I would like to pride myself on being like that as well."[4]

—JUSTIN TIMBERLAKE DESCRIBING TENNMAN RECORDS ARTIST MATT MORRIS

Matt Morris is a good friend of Timberlake's and one of the first artists Timberlake signed to his record label, Tennman Records.

and he even produced their recordings. Morris in particular was a friend of Timberlake's.

Timberlake wasn't finished. In 2009, he surprised the public by creating his own brand of tequila, a type of liquor. He named his brand 901, which was the telephone area code for his hometown of Memphis. While many critics expected it to be a poor-quality drink intended to simply capitalize on the singer's celebrity, many bar owners and tequila experts were surprised by the high quality of the upscale liquor.

Providing other celebrity endorsements would serve to keep Timberlake's name in the public eye and generate income for him. Timberlake even created a management company specifically for this aspect of his career: IMG Sports and Entertainment. Timberlake endorsed products such as Sony electronics, Audi automobiles, and the Givenchy men's fragrance Play.

Despite Timberlake's many different business ventures, in his heart he was still a musician. In 2009 he appeared at the Grammy Awards. He was supposed to perform one song that evening. Then the show's organizers received word that two of the other performers who were scheduled to sing on the show had suddenly pulled out. At

THE NEXT BIG THING

As part of his celebrity endorsement of Audi automobiles, Timberlake filmed a six-part miniseries for the car company that was available for viewing on the Internet. The Web series was filmed as a "suspense thriller," according to Audi.[5] Timberlake played John Frank, an information technology specialist who comes to the aid of Toni, a character played by actress Dania Ramirez.

the last minute—and with very little rehearsal time—Timberlake and famous soul singer Al Green performed the song "Let's Stay Together" with backup music provided by country musician Keith Urban and the R & B group Boyz II Men.

||||||||||||||||||||||||||||||||||||||||||||||||||||||||||||||||

DATING AND GOSSIP

While Timberlake was establishing his music, acting, and business careers, he was still a favorite of the Hollywood paparazzi and gossip columns because of his various personal relationships. He was linked with Britney Spears, Cameron Diaz, and actresses Alyssa Milano, Scarlett Johansson, and Jessica Biel. Timberlake and Diaz dated for nearly four years when rumors of infidelity on both sides led to their breakup in 2007. Rumors had plagued the couple throughout the course of their three-and-a-half-year relationship, but they kept silent about all of it.

"The worst thing about being famous is the invasion of your privacy."[6]

—*JUSTIN TIMBERLAKE*

Timberlake and Biel have been an on-again and off-again couple since 2007. Timberlake has said he enjoys dating other celebrities because they can relate to each other.

Like many show-business couples frequently profiled in the media, Timberlake's relationship with Diaz had suffered because of constant speculation and a lack of privacy. After dating Diaz, Timberlake was in a relationship with actress Jessica Biel. The relationship lasted several years, ending with a breakup in the early summer of 2011. However, in September 2011, Biel attended

In 2011, Timberlake told *Elle* magazine, "I would have made it without *NSYNC. I don't want this to come out the wrong way. It was an amazing platform but even without it, I believe I would have been heard as a solo artist."[8]

the Justin Timberlake Shriners Hospitals for Children Open along with Timberlake, fueling rumors that the pair was back together.

Timberlake discussed his romantic relationships and the effect of the paparazzi and constant media attention in an interview with *Vanity Fair* magazine:

> *Why do you think [celebrities] all like each other? Why do you think we wind up dating each other, and feeling more comfortable around each other? We understand what it's like. "Oh, thank God—finally, somebody who knows how I feel." It's refuge.*[7]

Despite his difficulties with personal relationships and the stress of his music, acting, and business endeavors, there was still more to Timberlake than being in the public eye and making money. As Timberlake approached his

With ventures in music, acting, philanthropy, and business, Timberlake's career is showing no signs of slowing down.

thirtieth birthday in 2011, it might have seemed that he had already done it all. He had achieved a successful music career in the band *NSYNC and as a solo performer, an acting career on television and in movies, and a reputation for his charitable contributions. But he was by no means ready to retire.

‖‖‖‖‖‖‖‖

Timberlake starred with Jesse Eisenberg, *right*, in *The Social Network*. It was one of the most critically acclaimed films of Timberlake's career.

CHAPTER 9

Still Inspired

||||||||||||||||||||||||||||||||||||||||||||||||||||||||||||||||||||||||||||||

By 2011, Timberlake was approaching his thirtieth birthday with many new moviemaking projects either completed or in the works. In 2009, he had been involved in *The Open Road* and was beginning to receive more encouraging reviews of his acting work. One reviewer called Timberlake "a born performer if not a great actor (at least not yet)."[1] But clearly his acting was being noticed. The magazine *Entertainment Weekly* had named him as one of their top 30 actors under age 30 for 2008.

||||||||||||||||||||||||||||||||||||||||||||||||||||||||||||||||||||||||||

FROM NAPSTER
TO TEACHER

Timberlake's movie project in 2010 was the biggest of his career, playing Napster founder Sean Parker in *The Social Network*. Timberlake's success in the role even spawned rumors that he might be nominated for an Academy Award in the Best Supporting Actor category, although it did not happen. One movie review Web site called him "one of the biggest pop stars in the world and, shockingly, he may be even better at acting than he is at singing."[2] Director David Fincher recalled auditioning Timberlake for the role of Parker. "[Parker] was described in the screenplay as moving through the room like Frank Sinatra," Fincher recalled. As Timberlake read for the part, Fincher was convinced he'd found his Sinatra. But, the director recalled, "Everyone thought he was too famous." In the end, Fincher's initial enthusiasm won out. Fincher said, "We finally decided, just because he's perfect doesn't mean we shouldn't cast him."[3]

After starring together in the 2011 film *Friends with Benefits*, there were rumors that Timberlake and Mila Kunis, *left*, were a couple.

Timberlake was definitely on his way to developing a major acting career. After *The Social Network*, he went on to provide the voice of Boo Boo in the animated movie *Yogi Bear*. In 2011, he took on several other major movie roles. His romantic comedy *Friends with Benefits*, which he starred in with actress Mila Kunis, received mostly good reviews. Timberlake's on-screen chemistry with Kunis was so strong, that many viewers and critics alike questioned if they were involved in real life—though both denied a romantic relationship.

It seemed to Timberlake's fans that he had put his music career on hold in favor of movie acting. Timberlake admitted that his music wasn't his first priority. In an interview with the magazine *Vanity Fair*, he said he realized that his career wouldn't only lie in music. He stated,

> *At first, I thought, Oh, man, people are going to think I'm the entitled guy who does music and then comes over to do movies, and I worried about things being misunderstood. . . . Film is much more communal, in both good and bad ways.*[4]

KUNIS DEFENDS TIMBERLAKE

During a press conference in Moscow, Russia, to publicize the movie *Friends with Benefits*, a Russian reporter asked Timberlake why he was acting instead of making more music. Kunis, Timberlake's costar, was offended by the question, which was asked in Russian—her native language. Kunis responded, "Why movies? Why not? What kind of question is that? Why are you here?" Timberlake did not receive a translation of the question until after Kunis spoke. He then pointed to Kunis and said, "This is my bodyguard."[5]

As Kunis and Timberlake were doing publicity for *Friends with Benefits*, they attracted some unusual military attention. Both stars were separately invited to attend a Marine Corps ball via YouTube videos. Corporal Kelsey De Santis invited Timberlake, and Sergeant Scott Moore asked Kunis. When Timberlake and Kunis attended the premiere of their movie in July, they each sent their dates on-camera messages from the red carpet.

Timberlake said, "Corporal, it's an honor. You frighten me a little bit, but I'm excited." The singer added, "I can't wait. What color corsage would you like?"

"Hello, Sergeant. I'm very excited," Kunis said. "I hope you're not disappointed."[7]

Timberlake's ball would take place in Washington DC on November 12, 2011, and Kunis's ball would be in North Carolina on November 18, 2011.

When asked if he was interested in making another music album Timberlake replied,

> I wouldn't say I'm not going to put out another one. I would say that would be a bad bet, if you were betting. But I could see myself only doing one more big tour.[6]

Timberlake has continued to be involved in television projects and occasionally hosts *Saturday Night Live* or awards shows such as the ESPN ESPY

Timberlake has hosted several awards shows in his recent career, including the ESPN ESPYs in 2008.

Awards. In August 2011, he appeared on the ABC television special "Science Is Rock and Roll" with other celebrities to promote a robotics competition and support science and technology education. He also continues to pursue his business interests, including the William Rast clothing line, and he

In 2011, Timberlake told *Vanity Fair* magazine that he was looking forward to promoting his upcoming movies. "It will be fun. I'll get to go to a bunch of countries, hang out. You know, where I'm at in my life, I'm alone and being in it, in each moment: good, bad, ugly, pretty—all of it, take it as it comes."[8]

recently invested in the company that purchased the social networking site MySpace.

|||||||||||||||||||||||||||||||||||||||||||||||||||||||||||

WHAT NEXT?

In the summer of 2011, Timberlake split his time between an apartment in the SoHo neighborhood of New York City and a luxury home in Los Angeles. He had broken up with his girlfriend Biel earlier that year, and despite rumors of a relationship with *Friends with Benefits* costar Kunis, he was not currently in another relationship.

Other than doing publicity for his newest movies, Timberlake was enjoying a break from a regimented schedule. He told an interviewer:

Right now, I'm not in the mood to work. . . . I want to not have a schedule. I want to go to the

Dodgers game if I feel like it. I've never really given myself the opportunity to be spontaneous. I figure I can go on like this until the end of the year. I don't have anything I have to do. The only job I have to do is promote the films that are coming out, and I'm really looking forward to that.[9]

But there's little doubt that Timberlake will continue to build both his acting and music careers in the future. When asked by a reporter if he ever intended to retire, he replied, "I don't know that I'll *ever* retire. I'll just find new things to inspire me."[10]

||||||||||

At 30 years old, Timberlake had already achieved success in music, acting, and business— it was anyone's guess where the next stage of his career would take him.

TIMELINE

1981

Justin Timberlake is born on January 31 in Memphis, Tennessee.

1993

Timberlake makes his first television appearance on the show *Star Search*.

1993

Timberlake joins the cast of *The All New Mickey Mouse Club* television show.

1998

In November, *NSYNC releases its second album titled *Home for Christmas*.

1999

Timberlake begins dating Britney Spears.

2000

On March 21, *NSYNC releases its third album, *No Strings Attached*.

1995	1995	1998
Timberlake auditions for boy band *NSYNC and becomes a member.	On October 22, *NSYNC gives their first performance.	*NSYNC releases its first US album, *NSYNC, on March 24.

2002	2002	2003
*NSYNC goes on hiatus in April and eventually disbands.	Timberlake releases his first solo album, Justified on November 5.	Timberlake begins dating actress Cameron Diaz.

TIMELINE

2003

On October 11, Timberlake hosts *Saturday Night Live* for the first time.

2004

Justified wins two Grammy Awards.

2006

In September, Timberlake releases *FutureSex/Love Sounds*.

2007

Timberlake opens a restaurant in New York City called Southern Hospitality.

2007

Timberlake begins dating Jessica Biel.

2008

Timberlake hosts and plays in the first annual The Justin Timberlake Shriners Hospitals for Children Open in October.

2006

2006

2007

Edison Force is released in the United States.

Timberlake and his friend Trace Ayala start a clothing line, William Rast.

Timberlake starts the Tennman Records label.

2009

2010

2011

Timberlake appears in a starring role in the movie *The Open Road*.

Timberlake portrays Napster founder Sean Parker in the Oscar-nominated movie *The Social Network*.

Timberlake has major roles in the movies *Bad Teacher*, *Friends with Benefits*, and *In Time*.

GET THE SCOOP

FULL NAME

Justin Randall Timberlake

DATE OF BIRTH

January 31, 1981

PLACE OF BIRTH

Memphis, Tennessee

ALBUMS

*NSYNC (1998), *Home for Christmas* (1998), *No Strings Attached* (2000), *Celebrity* (2001), *Justified* (2002), *FutureSex/LoveSounds* (2006)

SELECTED FILMS AND TELEVISION APPEARANCES

Edison Force (2006), *Alpha Dog* (2006), *The Open Road* (2009), *Saturday Night Live* (2003–2011), *The Social Network* (2010), *Yogi Bear* (2010), *Bad Teacher* (2011), *Friends with Benefits* (2011), *In Time* (2011)

SELECTED AWARDS

- Won 2004 Grammys for Best Male Pop Vocal Performance and Best Pop Vocal Album, *Justified* (2003)
- Won 2008 Grammys for Best Dance Recording and Best Rap/Sung Collaboration, *FutureSex/LoveSounds* (2007)

- Won Emmy for Outstanding Guest Actor in a Comedy Series for his appearance on *Saturday Night Live* (2009)
- Won Emmys for Outstanding Original Music and Outstanding Guest Actor in a Comedy Series for *Saturday Night Live* (2011)

BUSINESS

Timberlake has been partial owner of three restaurants. He co-owns clothing line William Rast with his friend Trace Ayala. He started his own record label, Tennman Records, and owns a golf course near Memphis. Timberlake has also provided endorsements for many different companies and products throughout the years.

PHILANTHROPY

Timberlake has created and supported multiple charities including Shriners Hospitals for Children and The Justin Timberlake Foundation. He is an avid supporter of music education through his own foundation and the Memphis Music Foundation. Timberlake also supports the environment. He owns an eco-friendly golf course and received the EMA Futures Award in 2011 for reducing his carbon footprint.

> **"I don't know that I'll ever retire. I'll just find new things to inspire me."**
>
> —*JUSTIN TIMBERLAKE*

GLOSSARY

audition—To give a trial performance showcasing personal talent as a musician, singer, dancer, or actor.

choreography—The arrangement of specific movements and steps for a dance.

collaborate—To work together in order to create or produce a work, such as a song or an album.

debut—A first appearance.

endorsement—A public approval or support for a product as a way to get other people to buy it.

hip-hop—A style of popular music associated with US urban culture that features rap spoken against a background of electronic music or beats.

infidelity—Unfaithfulness to a romantic partner.

philanthropy—An act of charity, such as a donation, for a humanitarian or environmental purpose.

producer—Someone who oversees or provides money for a play, television show, movie, or album.

rehearse—To practice something before a public performance.

sound mixing—The process during the postproduction stage of a film, music, or television program in which the collection of recorded sounds are combined and adjusted.

ADDITIONAL RESOURCES

SELECTED BIBLIOGRAPHY

Eliscu, Jenny. "The New King of Pop." *Rolling Stone* December 2003: 44–48. Print.

Grigoriadis, Vanessa. "A Free Man in L.A." *Vanity Fair*. Condé Nast Digital, July 2011. Web. 3 Oct. 2011.

JustinTimberlake.com. Tennman Entertainment. Web. 4 Oct. 2011.

Smith, Sean. *Justin: The Unauthorized Biography*. New York: Simon & Schuster, 2004. Print.

FURTHER READINGS

Boekhoff, Patti Marlene, and Stuart A. Kallen. **NSYNC*. San Diego: Kidhaven Press, 2003. Print.

Dougherty, Steve. *Justin Timberlake*. New York: Franklin Watts, 2009. Print.

Summers, Kimberly Dillon. *Justin Timberlake: A Biography*. Santa Barbara, CA: Greenwood, 2010. Print.

WEB SITES

To learn more about Justin Timberlake, visit ABDO Publishing Company online at **www.abdopublishing.com**. Web sites about Justin Timberlake are featured on our Book Links page. These links are routinely monitored and updated to provide the most current information available.

PLACES TO VISIT

Memphis Rock 'n' Soul Museum
191 Beale Street, Suite 100, Memphis, TN 38103
901-205-2533
www.memphisrocknsoul.org
This museum is dedicated to the history of the music and musicians of Memphis, Tennessee, Justin Timberlake's hometown.

Mirimichi Golf Course
6195 Woodstock Cuba Road, Millington, TN 38053
901-259-3800
www.mirimichi.com
Timberlake's eco-friendly golf course is open to the public.

Southern Hospitality BBQ
1460 Second Ave, New York, NY 10075
212-249-1001
www.southernhospitalitybbq.com/ue/
At the New York City barbeque restaurant Timberlake co-owns, some of the recipes used are based on Timberlake family recipes.

SOURCE NOTES

CHAPTER 1. IN THE SPOTLIGHT

1. Dan Simon. "Internet Pioneer Sean Parker: 'I'm Blazing a New Path.'" *CNNTech*. Turner Broadcasting System, Inc., 27 Sept. 2011. Web. 3 Oct. 2011.

2. K. C. Kelly. "Justin Timberlake Red Carpet Interview at 2011 Academy Awards." *Examiner.com*. Clarity Digital Group LLC, 27 Feb. 2011. Web. 3 Oct. 2011.

3. Leah Greenblatt. "Justin Timberlake's Going Back to the Studio!" *EW.com*. Entertainment Weekly Inc., 4 March 2011. Web. 3 Oct. 2011.

4. Kyle Anderson, "Justin Timberlake on his music career: 'I don't have a single song ready to go.'" *EW.com*. Entertainment Weekly Inc., 14 June 2011. Web. 3 Oct. 2011.

CHAPTER 2. TENNESSEE ROOTS

1. "J-14 Magazine Interviews with NSync's Moms!" *Justin Timberlake-Fan.com*. justintimberlake-fan.com, n.d. Web. 3 Oct. 2011.

2. Sean Smith. *Justin: The Unauthorized Biography*. New York: Simon & Schuster, 2004. Print. 32.

3. Ibid. 213.

CHAPTER 3. MOUSEKETEER TO MUSICIAN

1. "Scoop: The Mice That Roared Britney? 'N Sync? TV's Felicity? Matt Casella knew how to pick 'em." *People*. Time Inc., 7 Feb. 2000. Web. 3 Oct. 2011.

2. Vanessa Grigoriadis. "A Free Man in L.A." *Vanity Fair*. Condé Nast Digital, July 2011. Web. 3 Oct. 2011.

3. Ibid.

4. Danisha. "Lou Pearlman Likens Backstreet to Coke, *NSYNC to Pepsi." *Popdirt.com*. popdirt.com, 30 Oct. 2002. Web. 3 Oct. 2011.

5. Sean Smith. *Justin: The Unauthorized Biography*. New York: Simon & Schuster, 2004. Print. 88–89.

CHAPTER 4. *NSYNC

1. Vanessa Grigoriadis. "A Free Man in L.A." *Vanity Fair*. Condé Nast Digital, July 2011. Web. 3 Oct. 2011.

2. Ibid.

3. Ibid.

CHAPTER 5. A CHANGING ROLE

1. Nick Marino. "NSYNC Tour Opener: Dirty Pop And Matching Chaps." *MTV*. MTV Networks, 24 Mar. 2001. Web. 3 Oct. 2011.

2. Jenny Eliscu, "The New King of Pop." *Rolling Stone* Dec. 2003: 44–48. EBSCOhost. Web. 4 Oct. 2011.

3. Ibid.

4. Rosemary Ryan. "McDonald's Unveils New Global Campaign." *B&T*. Reed Business Information, 3 Sept. 2003. Web. 3 Oct. 2011.

CHAPTER 6. NEW DIRECTIONS

1. Ken Barnes. "Hive-Five Salute for Beyoncé." *USA Today*. Gannett Co. Inc., 9 Feb. 2004. Web. 3 Oct. 2011.

2. "Justin's Movie Effort Gets Thumbs Up from Onscreen Co-Stars." *hellomagazine.com*. HELLO!, 4 Jan 2007. Web. 3 Oct. 2011.

CHAPTER 7. USING HIS FAME FOR GOOD

1. Ron Cobb. "Justin Timberlake's Golf Course Is a Reason to Visit Memphis." *STLtoday*. STLtoday.com, 2 Jan. 2011. Web. 3 Oct. 2011.

2. "The Justin Timberlake Foundation Donates…" *PopSugar*. Sugar Inc., 23 Mar. 2008. Web. 3 Oct. 2011.

CHAPTER 8. TIMBERLAKE THE BUSINESSMAN

1. Kristin Chessman. "Not Just a Pretty Face." *Entrepreneur*. Entrepreneur Media, Inc. 17 Nov. 2008. Web. 3 Oct. 2011.

2. "Justin Timberlake's Race Car Wins Indy 500." *Today*. MSNBC. com, 30 May 2011. Web. 3 Oct. 2011.

SOURCE NOTES CONTINUED

3. Kristin Chessman. "Not Just a Pretty Face." *Entrepreneur*. Entrepreneur Media, Inc. 17 Nov. 2008. Web. 3 Oct. 2011.

4. "Chatting With Justin: The Artists of Tennman Records." *Justin Timberlake*. Tennman Entertainment, 5 Apr. 2009. Web. 3 Oct. 2011.

5. Alex Ricciuti. "Justin Timberlake & Audi A1 Star in 6 Episode Mini-Series." *WorldCarFan.com*. Black Falcon Media Group, 4 May 2010. Web. 3 Oct. 2011.

6. *BrainyQuote*. BookRags Media Network. 2011. Web. 3 Oct. 2011.

7. Vanessa Grigoriadis. "A Free Man in L.A." *Vanity Fair*. Condé Nast Digital, July 2011. Web. 3 Oct. 2011.

8. Tom Eames. "Justin Timberlake: 'I would have made it without *NSYNC.'" *Digital Spy*. National Magazine Company Ltd, 7 Aug. 11 2011. Web. 3 Oct. 2011.

CHAPTER 9. STILL INSPIRED

1. "Timberlake, Bridges Hit the Open Road." *Get The Big Picture*. Complex Media Network, 4 Aug. 2009. Web. 3 Oct. 2011.

2. "Why Justin Timberlake And His Social Network Co-Stars Deserve Oscars. *Cinemablend.com*. Cinema Blend LLC, 30 Sept. 2010. Web. 3 Oct. 2011.

3. Jonah Wiener. "Leading Man, Miles Beyond the Boy Band." *The New York Times*. The New York Times Company, 15 July 2011. Web. 3 Oct. 2011.

4. Vanessa Grigoriadis. "A Free Man in L.A." *Vanity Fair*. Condé Nast Digital, July 2011. Web. 3 Oct. 2011.

5. Scott Edward. "Mila Kunis chews out Russian reporter in Russian." *CBS News*. CBS Interactive Inc., 3 Aug. 2011. Web. 3 Oct. 2011.

6. Vanessa Grigoriadis. "A Free Man in L.A." *Vanity Fair*. Condé Nast Digital, July 2011. Web. 3 Oct. 2011.

7. Jessica Derschowitz. "Justin Timberlake, Mila Kunis Send Messages to Marine Dates." *CBS News*. CBS Interactive Inc., 20 July 2011. Web. 3 Oct. 2011.

8. Vanessa Grigoriadis. "A Free Man in L.A." *Vanity Fair*. Condé Nast Digital, July 2011. Web. 3 Oct. 2011.

9. Ibid.

10. Simon Vozick-Levinson. "What Goes Around…Comes Around." *EW.com*. Entertainment Weekly Inc., 21 June 2007. Web. 3 Oct. 2011.

INDEX

ABOUT THE AUTHOR

Marcia Amidon Lusted is the author of more than 60 books for young readers and hundreds of magazine articles. She is also an assistant editor for Cobblestone Publishing, a writing instructor, and a musician. She lives in New Hampshire with her family.

PHOTO CREDITS